Dzog Chen and Zen

Chögyal Namkhai Norbu was born in 1938 in Derghe, in Eastern Tibet and was recognized at birth as the reincarnation of a noted exponent of the Dzogchen tradition. Notwithstanding his youth, he was already well known by the end of the 1950s as a person with a profound knowledge of the Dzogchen teachings and also as a spiritual teacher. His fame in India and in Tibet was such that in 1960 Professor Giuseppe Tucci, an eminent scholar and founder of the Is. MEO (one of the major institutes of oriental studies in Italy), invited him to Rome to collaborate in research at what is today known as Is.I.A.O, (Istituto per l'Africa e l'Oriente). It was thus that Namkhai Norbu came to Italy where he contributed actively in the development of Tibetan studies in the West.

In 1962 he took up a post teaching Tibetan language and literature in Naples at the Istituto Universitario Orientale di Napoli where he worked until 1992.

For the first fifteen years of his residence in Italy, Namkhai Norbu concentrated mainly on the Ancient History of Tibet. His works are evidence of his deep knowledge of Tibetan culture and are addressed to the young people of Tibet in order that their awareness of an ancient cultural heritage should not die out. The works of Namkhai Norbu are a significant reference point for these young people, whether they live in the People's Republic of China or whether they are living in exile, and represent the continuation of the cultural heritage of Tibet and its national identity. His studies have become so well known at an international level that he has an intense program of lectures and seminars in the major centers of Oriental studies and in universities throughout the world.

From the mid-seventies Namkhai Norbu began to teach Yantra Yoga and Dzogchen meditation to a few Italian students, and the growing interest in his teachings convinced him to dedicate himself increasingly to such activities. Together with a number of disciples he founded the first Dzogchen community in Arcidosso in Tuscany and then later founded other centers in various parts of Europe, Russia, the United States, South America, and Australia. To connect with the Dzogchen community over the internet, go to http://www.dzogchen.it

Namkhai Norbu

Dzog Chen
and
Zen

Edited
with a Preface and Notes
by Kennard Lipman

Blue Dolphin Publishing
1986

Published by Blue Dolphin Publishing, Inc.
P.O. Box 8, Nevada City, CA 95959
Orders: 1-800-643-0765
Web: www.bluedolphinpublishing.com

ISBN: 0-931892-08-2
LCCN: 94-131023

*Cover: A Chinese-Tibetan lexicon, ca. 9th century,
Dunhuang. P.T. 1257.*

Printed in the United States of America

10   9   8   7   6

Table of Contents

Preface

This lecture by Namkhai Norbu, professor of Tibetan and Mongolian Languages and Literatures at the Istituto Orientale of the University of Naples, Italy, was originally given at the University of California, Berkeley, on July 2, 1981. In it Professor Norbu discusses the relationship between Zen (Chinese: Ch'an) and Zógqen (rDzogs chen) in the context of the encounter, during the seventh to ninth centuries, between Chinese Ch'an Buddhists and the various currents of exoteric (sutric) and esoteric (tantric) Buddhism developing in Tibet. This was the period of the initial spread of Buddhism in Tibet. In particular, Professor Norbu focuses on the Zógqen teaching, regarded by its followers as the pinnacle of Buddhist teachings. In this preface I wish primarily to outline the Tibetan approach to grading the levels of Buddhist practice which Professor Norbu has utilized.

Understanding the relation of the Zógqen system to Zen is very much a contemporary issue. In the West, the Tibetan and Zen forms of Buddhism continue to be the most widespread forms to be seriously practiced. This is no accident, for both Zógqen and Zen have managed to maintain some semblance of vitality despite many centuries of decline of Buddhism in Asia. This is due, at least in part, to the fact that both are "direct," non-gradual approaches to the Buddhist teaching, and represent in this sense the culminations of Tantric and Sutric Buddhism, respectively. In Western (and Japanese) academic circles, research into the issue of "sudden" versus "gradual" awakening, and the roles of Indian and Chinese Buddhism in early Tibet, have been given new impetus recently by detailed studies on the relevant Dunhuang documents, especially by Japanese scholars. Also, the *Sàmdan Migdrön* (*bSam gtan mig sgron*, see below, n. 11, 12), an extremely important authentic source for this issue and period, has recently been published.

The *Sàmdan Migdrön* clearly and precisely distinguishes the gradual, sutric approach of Kamalaśīla, the great Indian master;

5

the non-gradual sutric approach of Haxañ (*Ha shang*) Mahāyāna, the principal representative of Chinese Ch'an Buddhism in early Tibet; the Tantrism of the Mahāyoga system of what came later to be known as the Ñiñmaba (rNying ma pa) tradition of Tibetan Buddhism; and finally, Atiyoga, or Zógqen, introduced into Tibet by masters such as Padmasambhava, Vimalamitra, and Vairocana. Understanding these distinctions is the key to understanding the relation of Zógqen to Zen.

A gradual path considers it necessary to slowly progress through a series of stages in order to reach the goal, "enlightenment." The individual is viewed as possessing grosser and subtler impediments to manifesting this enlightenment; the impediments must be tackled step by step, from grosser to more subtle, primarily through the application of appropriate antidotes. This progression is epitomized in the "Five Paths": there is a preparatory stage (*sambhāramārga*) of accumulating the requisites for this long journey, which links up (*prayogamārga*) to a direct insight into oneself and reality (*darśanamārga*) that eliminates the impediments which can be eliminated by insight alone. But there are also subtler impediments which must be removed by repeated attention to them on the stage of cultivation (*bhāvanāmārga*), which fundamentally consists of the Eight-fold Noble Path. In the Mahāyāna, the ten stages of the Bodhisattva are said to be traversed through the training in the so-called "perfections" (*pāramitā*) of generosity, ethical behavior, strenuousness, patience, meditative concentration, and discernment. Finally one reaches the stage of "No More Learning" (*aśaikṣamārga*), the goal, Buddhahood. It is said that the Bodhisattva practices in this way for three eons in order to reach the goal.

On this gradual path the Bodhisattva always attempts to combine compassion, as appropriate action (operating on the level of relative truth) with the discernment of emptiness, *śūnyatā* (operating on the level of absolute truth). Furthermore, the meditative practices of calm (*śamatha*) and insight (*vipaśyanā*) are also practiced in a gradual manner, focusing on different topics. In particular, insight is developed in a rather intellectual style through, first, study, then reasoning about what one has studied, and finally, meditative experience of the matter at hand. As mentioned below (p. 24) by Professor Norbu, Kamalaśīla's *Bhāvanākrama* (*The Stages of Cultivation*), was composed as an authoritative guide to the gradual path for the Tibetans.

The non-gradual approach recognizes that the root of all impediments is dualism and that dualism can only be cut through directly, with all of one's efforts constantly directed towards this radical cure. This leads to a kind of meditative practice, such as *zazen*, which proceeds to immediately unify calm and insight, appropriate action and discernment.[1] Also, in this approach, intellectual study and reasoning about *śūnyatā* are not considered necessary prerequisites to its direct, meditative understanding. Here, in this directness, lies the similarity between Zen and Zógqen.

We may sum up these gradual and non-gradual sutra teachings with the famous verse of Nāgārjuna's *Mūlamadhyamakakārikā*, his fundamental work (Ch. 18, v. 5):

> By the destruction of the passions and the karmic acts (which result from them), liberation comes about.
> Passions and karmic acts come from conceptual fictions.
> These spread from the (dualistic) naming activity of the mind, which is halted by *śūnyatā*.

The gradual and non-gradual traditions represent, then, more or less rapid, i.e., direct, approaches to the realization of *śūnyatā*; this directness depends on the "spiritual acumen," the sharpness of the individual's faculties. It must be remembered that the sutras are based primarily on a principle of renunciation or elimination of obstacles. In this sense then, *śūnyatā*, the fact that nothing possesses an exhaustively specifiable and unvarying mode of being, is the supreme antidote for the follower of the sutras. Thus, Professor Norbu, following the *Sàmdan Migdrön*, has spoken below (p. 26) of the way in which the sutric practitioner is always "aiming at" *śūnyatā*, the ultimate truth. Furthermore, we can also see why the ideal sutric practitioner almost always has been the monk, Zen included.

Zen, like the teaching of the "Buddha-nature" (*tathāgata-*

garbha) inherent in all sentient beings, represents for the Tibetan tradition a kind of transition to Tantrism. In such transitional teachings, an understanding of *śūnyatā* which goes beyond the antidotal approach, is opened up. In such an understanding, *śūnyatā* manifests itself very positively; it is not merely an antidote. Thus, the *Sàmdan Migdrön* goes on to explain the superiority of Tantrism to the non-gradual teaching of Haxañ Mahāyāna. It is considered superior because its method is superior. In Tantrism the passions are transformed through visualization and through manipulation of the bodily energies which are their support. This method is considered much more rapid than that of applying antidotes. It, in fact, presupposes the "antidotal" understanding of *śūnyatā* mentioned above; that is, an ego-centered, complacent attitude towards the world (which *śūnyatā* counters) inhibits one from imaginatively varying one's experience to the extent of seeing oneself as a divine being in a *maṇḍala*-palace, a central practice of Tantrism. In tantric terms, *śūnyatā* is also a radiant presence full of vivid imagery; by developing experience of this presence the passions can be transformed into their pristine state, which is clarity and insight. Here the passions are neither avoided nor ignored, but are rather welcomed, even accentuated, in order to be transformed. Needless to say, such an approach requires a rather special and precise method; hence its esoteric and "secret" character.

We may explain this difference between the teachings of the sutras and tantras in another way, not in terms of how they understand the absolute reality, *śūnyatā*, but in terms of how they view the relative reality of our sense-based experience. In the sutras the relative reality, summed up by our five psychophysical constituents (*skandha*), is always seen as something "impure." It is our ordinary world, subject and object of either like, dislike, or indifference. It was in this sense that we spoke above of our normal ego-centered, complacent attitude. In the tantras, on the other hand, this relative reality is seen as something primordially "pure" and transparent. In this trans-figured vision, the five *skandhas*, as subject, are the Buddhas of the five "families," while the five elements, earth, fire, etc., as object, are their five feminine counterparts, with whom they

8

are in blissful union. This transfigured vision, however, requires immense effort and concentration. The lower tantras, for example, place great emphasis on purification ("When the gates of perception are cleansed, everything will be seen as it is: infinite") in order to achieve this transformation. The higher tantras rely more directly on the individual's capacity for visualization and for working with one's subtle bodily energies.

The *Sàmdan Migdrŏn* goes on to explain the superiority of Atiyoga or Zógqen to this tantric way of transformation. There is much confusion about the relation of Zógqen to Tantrism. In the system of the Ñiñmaba school, for example, there is a nine-fold division of spiritual pursuits (*yāna*). There are the three ordinary or common pursuits of the sutras: that of gods and men (a worldly path which leads merely to a better rebirth through virtuous conduct, for example), that of the Śrāvakas and Pratyekabuddhas (the so-called Hinayāna), and that of the Bodhisattvas of the Mahāyāna. Then there are the three outer tantras: Kriyā, Caryā, and Yoga. Finally there are the three inner, unsurpassable pursuits: Mahāyoga, Anuyoga, and Ati-yoga. As indicated above, the three ordinary pursuits primarily teach the way of renunciation (*poñ lam, spong lam*), the three outer tantras primarily the way of purification (*jyòñ lam, sbyong lam*), and the three inner tantras primarily the way of transformation (*gyúr lam, sgyur lam*). It would seem from this scheme that Atiyoga, Zógqen, belongs to the path of trans-formation, but this is not so. Zógqen is not based on a principle of transformation through *maṇḍala* practice, but on that of intrinsic freedom, self-liberation (*rañ drŏl, rang grol*). It teaches that the primordial state of the individual, usually termed *rig ba* (*rig pa, vidyā**) or *jyāñqub sem* (*byang chub sems, bodhicitta*), is a spontaneously-generating great *maṇḍala* in which nothing is lacking. By understanding this, passions and karmic actions are naturally freed just at and where they arise, without there being anything to reject or any means of rejection. Thus, it encompasses the path of renunciation. Since this primordial state of being can never be tainted by the passions and the karmic actions which stem from them, just as the surface of a mirror is unchanged by whatever images may appear in it, there is nothing to be purified nor any agent of purification. Thus, it

9

encompasses the path of purification. Also, since in this primordial condition striving to acquire a transfigured vision of the world also has come to an end, there is nothing to be transformed nor anything to do the transformation. Thus, it encompasses the way of transformation. Hence, the terms "spontaneously perfect" (*lhun drub, lhun grub*), "great primordial purity" (*gadăg qenbo, ka dag chen po*), "state of total completeness" (*Zógqen*), "state of pure and total presence" (*jyăñqubsem, byang chub sems*) are used. The word "tantra" also ultimately refers to this state which is the primordial, inalienable condition of the individual's own stream of awareness. The tantras of the way of transformation, however, primarily employ special methods, such as deity, *mantra, mudrā, samaya*, etc., in order to accomplish this transformation. Zógqen's special method, on the other hand, is intrinsic freedom, self-liberation.

We hope that Professor Norbu's lecture will serve as a useful introduction to the issues raised by a comparison of these different systems of Buddhist thought and practice. Future research will have to take a look at Zógqen in relation to Zen in its mature forms in China, Korea, and Japan, where it had contact with, and often incorporated aspects of, Tantrism as well as the all-encompassing, complete (*yuan*) doctrine of the Huayen tradition.

The term *Zen* has been used in the title of this work only because it is more well known than its Chinese original, Ch'an. This lecture is actually a discussion of Ch'an Buddhism in Tibet during a period before it ever reached Japan or even fully matured in China. The lecture well reflects the fact that the author wears two hats, one as professor of Tibetan and Mongolian Languages at the Istituto Orientale, University of Naples, Italy, and the other as meditation master in the Zógqen tradition. Thus, I have added footnotes, mostly of a scholarly nature, documenting important points relating to the principal topic of Zógqen and Zen. I have also included parts of the lecture in the footnotes, such as portions of answers to questions. In the introduction and body of the text I have utilized the transcription system for Tibetan developed and used for many years in Italy by Professor Norbu, followed by the Wylie romanization where the word first occurs. Today

10

there is no universally accepted system for transcribing spoken Tibetan. There are many *ad hoc* systems to be found in both scholarly and non-scholarly books; the problem is complicated when one does not know what dialect might be involved. Professor Norbu, on the other hand, has developed a rational system based on the Pinyin system for Chinese currently used by the People's Republic and in most academic circles. Since the footnotes are mainly intended for those with more scholarly interest in the subject matter, I have only used there the standard Wylie romanization for Tibetan. An advantage of Professor Norbu's system is that, in addition to providing a simpler guide to pronunciation than that of Goldstein,[2] for example, it is also fairly easily converted into Tibetan spelling by the specialist who familiarizes him or herself with it. A guide to the system follows this Preface. A concession to current usage is made, however, in the transcription of *rDzogs chen* as Dzog chen, instead of Zógqen, in the title.

The lecture was originally given in Italian and translated at that time by Barrie Simmons.

Dr. *Kennard Lipman*
Berkeley, California

Notes:

1. The famous *Platform Sutra*, ascribed to Hui-neng, the 6th Patriarch of Ch'an states: "Good and learned friends, calmness and wisdom are the foundations of my method. First of all, do not be deceived into thinking that the two are different. They are one substance and not two. Calmness is the substance of wisdom and wisdom is the function of calmness. Whenever wisdom is at work, calmness is within it. Whenever calmness is at work, wisdom is within it" (*The Platform Scripture*, Wing-tsit Chan, tr., New York: St. John's University Press, 1963, p. 45).
2. Goldstein, M.C., & Nornang, N. *Modern Spoken Tibetan* (Seattle: University of Washington Press, 1970).

Guide to Pronunciation

1. This symbol ˇ indicates a low tone.
2. This symbol ˋ indicates a nasalization before the immediately preceeding consonant (as in ingot).
3. This symbol ´ indicates a stress in the pronunciation.

Tibetan spelling		English sound	Tibetan spelling		English sound
Ga	-	karma	Na	-	nine
Gǎ	-	karma, low tone	Nà	-	nine, nasalized
Gà	-	singable, nasalized	Ná	-	nine, stressed
Gá	-	gale, stressed	Ña	-	ring
			Ñà	-	ring, nasalized
Ja	-	chant	Ñá	-	ring, stressed
Jǎ	-	chant, low tone	Ña	-	onion
Jà	-	angel, nasalized	Ñà	-	onion, nasalized
Já	-	jade, stressed	Ñá	-	onion, stressed
Da	-	tantra	Ma	-	man
Dǎ	-	tantra, low tone	Mà	-	man, nasalized
Dà	-	standard, nasalized	Má	-	man, stressed
Dá	-	day, stressed	Ka	-	kha, aspirated
Ba	-	path	Kà	-	as above, nasalized
Ba	-	path, low tone	Qa	-	channel, with strongly aspirated h
Bà	-	amber, nasalized			
Bá	-	banner, stressed	Qà	-	channel, nasalized
Sa	-	sand	Ta	-	aspirated, t-ha
Sǎ	-	sand, low tone	Tà	-	nasalized, nt-ha
Sà	-	sand, stressed	Pa	-	aspirated, p-ha
Sá	-	usual	Pà	-	nasalized, np-ha
Xa	-	shore	Ca	-	ts-ha, aspirated
Xǎ	-	shore, low tone	Cà	-	nasalized, nts-ha
Xà	-	shore, stressed	Ya	-	yes
Xá	-	jour	Yá	-	yes, stressed
Za	-	cats	Ra	-	rainbow
Zǎ	-	words	Rá	-	rainbow, stressed
Zà	-	words, nasalized			
Zá	-	words, stressed			

Tibetan spelling		English sound	Tibetan spelling		English sound
La	-	light	**Vowels**		
Lá	-	light, stressed	A	-	allah
Wa	-	water	I	-	me
Wá	-	water, stressed	U	-	moon
Va	-	water, low tone	E	-	way
Ha	-	hut	O	-	ore
Hă	-	soundless h, vowel in low tone	**Final consonants, preceded by a vowel**		
Gya	-	kiosk	-g	-	back
Gyă	-	kiosk, low tone	-ñ	-	ring
Gyà	-	gya, nasalized	-b	-	trip (lightly)
Gyá	-	gya, stressed	-m	-	hum
Jya	-	chya, non-aspirated	-s	-	soundless, changes the preceding vowel
Jyă	-	chya, low tone			1. as - e in met
Jyà	-	jya, nasalized			2. is - e in me
Jyá	-	jya, stressed			3. us - German ü
Kya	-	k aspirated + y, khya			4. es - é in René
Kyà	-	aspirated, nasalized			5. o - German ö
Qya	-	cha, aspirated	-d	-	cat, vowels change as with -s
Qyà	-	ncha, nasalized	-n	-	pen, vowels change as with -s
Dra	-	translation			
Dră	-	translation, low tone	-r	-	car (lightly, the vowel lengthens)
Drà	-	translation, nasalized			
Drá	-	translation, stressed	-l	-	fill, vowels change as with -s
Tra	-	t-hra, aspirated			
Trà	-	nt-hra, aspirated			
Lha	-	hla			
Hra	-	hra			

Dzog Chen and Zen

In regard to the Zógqen teaching, I'd like to first say a few words about its origin and history, before going on to the relation between it and Zen (Chinese: Ch'an). It is important as regards any given country to understand its historicial origins. In this case, that of Tibet, its historical origins are much more importantly linked to Bŏn than Buddhism. Scholars of Tibetan history, above all those of the Buddhist tradition, have chosen to ignore this set of facts; they have sought, as much as possible, to eliminate from history the origins of Tibet in the Bŏn. If we were to continue this, what would happen, particularly today when Tibet is under Chinese rule? Tibet's history and culture are in the situation of a lamp in the wind. I am not making anti-Chinese propaganda here. We all know that today Tibet is within China. Even if the Chinese were to take care of Tibet as if it were their son, we know that China is close to arriving at a population of one billion while the Tibetans are a few million. Furthermore, no one exists permanently. Thus, the only possibility of avoiding the complete cancellation, abolition of Tibetan history, is that of trying sincerely to conserve some values. In this case, for example, if one is performing scholarly work, one has to attempt to find what the value is that requires preservation. Through this search for values, we come upon the fact that the history that does exist has its origins in Bŏn. Unfortunately, people always wake up too late. I remember in my youth, in Tibet, after about two years of being in China, when I returned to my homeland, I understood clearly already what had to happen in Tibet if it were to avoid what eventually happened. I spoke to many people, above all to the monks, urging them to begin some process of change on their own. I had seen in Shanghai a Buddhist association where many monasteries had put their capital together and organized a kind of factory where they sent the young monks to work and earn

14

their living. Thus they had found a device for maintaining their existence under the guidance of the Communist Party in China. It was also a device for protecting the capital of the monasteries against the danger of the revolution. I spoke about this to the monasteries and particularly urged it on the rich monasteries. The only response of the monks and of the monasteries was, "You've become a Communist." Only later, once they had fled to India, did these people understand that what I had said to them was useful. And they would ask me, "And now what can we do?" This is an example.

Zógqen is usually presented as the highest teaching of the Ñiñmaba (rNying ma pa) school of Tibetan Buddhism. Tibetan Buddhists have their own private and rather limited vision of things. According to Tibetan Buddhists, Zógqen is something that belongs to the Ñiñmaba school; therefore, whoever teaches or practices Zógqen is automatically considered to belong to the Ñiñmaba school. But this is, in fact, the limited outlook of the schools. They do not want to know and understand, for example, that the Zógqen teaching also exists independently in the Bŏn tradition.[1] All of the Tibetan Buddhist historians repetitively recite the statement that the Zógqen which exists in the Bŏn school has been taken from the Ñiñmaba teachings. They also say, for example, that the various teachers in the Bŏn school who had taught Zógqen were emanations of Buddhist figures.

This is something that is very important for us to look at. First of all, as regards the Zógqen teaching, there is no importance given to whether it is Buddhist or not. What is most important is to know whether the Zógqen teaching is, or is not, a key for transcending our limited, dualistic condition. This has nothing to do with methods that are particularly Bŏnbo (Bon po) or Ñiñmaba or whatever, but rather a principle of the Zógqen teaching. Nor is it something necessarily limited to Zógqen, but could be true of other teachings. For example, when we speak of Buddhists in general, we have to understand that all the limitations of schools are created by men. The schools of Zen Buddhism, Theravāda, Tantrism, or Zógqen

15

may be presented in diverse fashions, but these diverse ways of presenting the teaching each deal with different individuals and what these individuals feel, think, and believe. But as for the principle of the teaching, we know, for example, that Buddha never created any schools. Man does not want to understand this. A human being has his limits. And thus in every conceivable way, with every possible means, he tries to make the teaching enter into his own limits. When we speak of a certain kind of school, we are always speaking of something presented within its limitations. Thus, the teaching can exist at many levels, in many different traditions. We can find the Zógqen teaching in the Bŏnbo school, but this does not mean that Zógqen is Bŏnbo. What it does mean is that Zógqen is a principle of the teaching, a key for transcending our limitations.

Let us take a look at the early history of Tibetan Buddhism, beginning back in the time of the King Sòñzan Gámbo (Srong btsan sgam po) in the seventh century. We know that Bŏn did not begin in that period. We know that Bŏn began long before the beginnings of the Tibetan monarchy. The person we call the king Sòñzan Gámbo was, according to Buddhist and Bŏn sources, the thirty-third king of Tibet. It was said that the Tibetan monarchy began with the king Ñátri Zanbo (gNya'khri btsan po).[2] We know that before the king Ñátri Zanbo there already had existed a famous Bŏnbo who was called Nàñvai Dògjan (sNang ba'i mdog can), who had been like a sustainer or spokesman of the population of what we now call Tibet.[3] In that period there was not even the name, Kingdom of Tibet, but even this is not the beginning. Long before that, there had been the kingdom of Xăñxŭñ (Zhang Zhung) in the western part of what we now call Tibet. In this area we find the area later called Guge where Mount Kailasa and a lake called Manasarovar are located, from which are said to flow the Ganges, Brahmaputra, and so forth. The Indians, or Hindus, considered this a most holy place. That was the location of the capital of the then kingdom of Xăñxŭñ. One of the first kings of Xăñxŭñ, who was called Triyer (Khri yer), lived three or four hundred years before the historical Buddha Śākyamuni, according to Bŏn sources. During the reign of that king, the first official Bŏn teacher lived and flourished.

In that period before the introduction of Buddhism, there already existed a type of Zógqen teaching, the *Xăńxŭń Ñàngyúd (Zhang Zhung snyan brgyud)*, or the oral teachings of Xăńxŭń.[4] This teaching was later introduced into the rest of Tibet in the period of the king Sòńzan Gámbo. How can we understand that this happened in the time of Sòńzan Gámbo? We know that it was in that time because the history of this teaching speaks of the period of the king Ligmigya (Lig mi rkya) of Xăńxŭń, and that this king Ligmigya was assassinated by the Tibetans. Having killed him, the Tibetans then took over the kingdom of Xăńxŭń. That piece of history we find in the Dunhuang documents, and we know that the Dunhuang documents are considered by all scholars to be authentic.[5] So we know that there did exist this *Xăńxŭń Ñàngyúd*, the oral teaching of Xăńxŭń. If one says that this *Xăńxŭń Ñàngyúd*, that is, an oral Zógqen teaching in the Bŏn school, exists, and then thinks automatically, "Ah, Zógqen came from Xăńxŭń," this is not the point. One must not think that Zógqen is like a book that is written first in such and such a place. We find, for example, in one of the tantras of Zógqen, it is said that the Zógqen teaching is found in thirteen different solar systems. How can we possibly then think that Zógqen originated in a given country and is the result of happenings in that particular location?

Furthermore, since the Buddhist schools all have a rather limited vision, whenever they speak of a given Buddhist teaching, they try to associate it, for example, with a specific saying or statement of the historical Buddha Śākyamuni. This is a very limited way of looking at things. The principle is not that. If that were the principle, it would be more than sufficient to follow something like the Theravāda tradition of sutric Buddhism, because what Buddha Śākyamuni taught orally to people was something like sutric Buddhism. It was not even the sutric Buddhism of the Mahāyāna Sutras; we know very well that Mahāyāna Buddhism developed later. In this way we would have to think of the most authentic teaching of Buddha as just the Vinaya. But the principle is not that. What we have to

17

understand is that there are many, many dimensions of the teaching. When we speak of a realized being, we need not think that only Buddha Śākyamuni achieved realization. We must not forget to think of what we speak of as the Tathāgatas, or what are spoken of as the thousand Buddhas. There exist many, many ways for realized beings to manifest themselves and for the teaching to arise.

As regards Tantrism, for example, we find that every tantra has its moment of appearance and its particular history. We must not imagine that Buddha Śākyamuni was like an actor, though many people think of him in that way. When they speak of the *Guhyasamāja Tantra*, it is as if Buddha had arrived in Odiyana and performed a kind of manifestation, did a show. When they speak of the *Kālacakra*, it is as if the Buddha had continued his tour there and put on another show; in this way almost all Tantrism is attributed to Buddha Śākyamuni as he travels about.[6] This is a typically human way of seeing things. The truth is, we find many aspects to the dimension of realization: it does not mean that all realized beings fuse into one being. It does mean that all these realized beings exist at the same level of capacity, the same kind of power. In this case many, many types of manifestation can exist at different moments. Thus you can understand that a given teaching may have existed thousands of years ago and may have come into being in different places. For example, take the form, the appearance of the divinities as they occur in Tantrism. All of them are relative to given conditions and times. It is obvious that, when we speak of realization, realization does not have some particular form. But it does take on a form for someone who understands, for one to whom it appears; yet this person has his limitations and perceives only in a limited way. Thus, you can perfectly well understand that the teaching and its origins do not have some specific and limited locations.

As regards Zógqen in the Buddhist tradition, we know that it was introduced primarily in the time of Padmasambhava, when the king Trisoñ Dézan ruled in Tibet. One of the most famous disciples of Padmasambhava was Vairocana. Vairocana had also been in India. He probably had also been in Odiyana, although we are not sure of that. He was responsible for the major part of the introduction of the Zógqen teaching in Tibet. The Zógqen teachings which were introduced by Vairocana exist primarily in two series, the *Semdé (Sems sde)* and *Lóndé (Klong sde)*.[7] Today when people usually speak of Zógqen, they use *Semdé* and *Lóndé* as if they were just names, always basing the teaching concretely on the *Upadeśa* series, or *Mannagdé (Man ngag sde)*.[8] The *Upadeśa* is, above all, the most essential part of the teaching, as well as being those instructions given as a specific method by master to disciple. There also exists what we speak of as the tradition of the *derma (gter ma)*, which means a teaching that has been hidden and later, perhaps rediscovered by someone. Much of this *Upadeśa* series comes from the *derma*. In Tibet, in particular, the principle of *derma* was extremely precise. The motivation had been to maintain or conserve the authentic teaching. A kind of person like Padmasambhava is considered to possess knowledge of what might happen in the future. It is said that Padmasambhava hid many important elements of the teaching to prevent their being destroyed by the evil kings of Tibet. This was true not only of Padmasambhava but of many other masters who, foreseeing difficult times, hid the teachings. In many of these cases, after the negative conditions had passed, the teachings were rediscovered.

We also have many discussions of the problems of authenticity as regards the *derma*. Many people do not believe they exist, others do. The principle is not believing or disbelieving. The principle is to know and understand what the substance of the teaching is. It is not the case that a teaching discovered and found in the form of *derma* is a complete novelty. As regards the teaching of Zógqen, all of the texts of the *Semdé* and *Lóndé* series have always been considered authentic and unquestionable. In the *Upadeśa*, also the best known are seventeen tantras which were said to have been discovered by a *derdon* who was called Dońma Lúngyál (Dong ma lhun rgyal). They had been hidden by a disciple of Vimalamitra, called Deñzin Sàñbo (Ting 'dzin bzang po).[9] He was a very, very famous master. Many people imagine that until those seven-

dGa' rab rdo rje, the first master of rDzogs chen, received the teaching in a visionary transmission from Vajrasattva, the Saṃbhogakāya aspect of Buddhahood. Many of his works are preserved in the Tibetan Tripiṭaka, although the dates of his life are in dispute.

Bodhidharma, the founder of Ch'an, was said to have transmitted this teaching from India in a lineage ultimately going back to Śākyamuni. None of his works survive and many scholars question his historicity.

teen tantras had been discovered, this teaching did not exist. But this is not true since, even in the absence of these texts, the oral lineage had continued to exist, as is explained in the historical texts. This means that the *derma* are not something entirely new coming to light. The discovery of these *derma* is thus very important to verify whether there have been changes in the teaching in the course of time. The origins of the Buddhist Zógqen are all of this order. It is not a matter of just a few but of many, many books.

Now what is the difference between the teaching of Zógqen and other teachings? One can describe precisely the differences in method that differentiate Zógqen, Tantrism in general, and the sutric level of Buddhism. One mode of easily understanding the differences is to look at the path that is involved, the way to realization. Here you can speak of the path of renunciation of the sutras, the path of transformation of the tantras, and the path of self-liberation of Zógqen. Clearly, if we read a Buddhist sutra for example, one can also find the Zógqen teaching within it, if one clearly understands the principle of Zógqen. But if one has not understood, then in order to arrive at this knowledge everything depends on the method employed, and for this reason the methods used may be different. In the Buddhist sutras, fundamentally the method used is that of renunciation. This is true of all of the different schools of sutric Buddhism, whether it be Theravāda, or the school of Zen Buddhism, or the Mahāyāna Buddhism of the followers of Nāgārjuna. In this approach, the first action, the first gesture of those who present themselves as Buddhists is, for example, to take refuge. When we take refuge, there is, above all, something negative which we have renounced. It is sufficient, for example, to think about the fact that in taking refuge one receives a name. Why does one have to receive a name, if you are already born with a name? This is a way of expressing, of exemplifying, that one is renouncing one's prior life and how one was. If one goes a step further, the best way of living in this life is held to be monkhood; if one wishes to truly sustain and support the teaching, one should become a monk, it is said. If one gives such importance to being a monk, what is the reason? The monk is the example of renunciation of all that is worldly.

In regard to overcoming all kinds of negativity, the method here is one of renunciation through the application of an antidote, such as compassion applied to hatred.

There are two modes of applying this principle: one is a more gradual path, the other is a more direct approach. When we speak of proceeding gradually, we talk about what sutric Buddhism in Tibet, among others, taught in the time of Padmasambhava, for example. It is obvious that Padmasambhava was not a great sutric master. What Padmasambhava taught was the Vajrayāna. Before the Vajrayāna emerged, there had already been a Chinese Buddhist master referred to by the Tibetans as Haxañ (Ha shang) Mahāyāna. The way of presenting and understanding Buddhism in China was quite different from that of Tibetan Buddhists. It is said that from China came the first master who introduced Buddhism in Tibet. One of the most ancient histories of Tibet says that there was a master who had been called Bodhidharmottara, that his master had been a disciple of a lineage going back to Kāśyapa.[10] Kāśyapa had been a disciple of Buddha Śākyamuni. It is said that Haxañ had received the "complete" teaching of the sutras. Here there is an interesting concept: what is called the "complete sutra" and the "incomplete sutra" teachings.[11] But Tibetan Buddhists officially do not accept this theme, since they became rather opposed to this teacher Haxañ.

In the time of Padmasambhava there was a great disciple of his, Nubqen Sañgyás Yexes (gNubs chen sangs rgyas ye shes), who had written a very, very beautiful book, the *Sàmdan Migdrön (Bsam gtan mig sgron)*.[12] Sàmdan means "contemplation," and Migdrön means "the light of the eyes." It is one of the most important texts on the Zógqen teachings, but it is not a tantra. It is written by that teacher, a human author. It could be said that this is the one text that clearly explains the difference between the Chinese tradition of Buddhism, the Zógqen teaching, the Tibetan Mahāyāna, and Tantrism. It is important, first of all, because the teacher who wrote this book was completely outside all of the limitations and arguments of the schools. He was a master who had realized the knowledge of

Zógqen. Secondly, he was a master who had had direct knowledge and contact with each of these schools. For example, in Tibet there are many, many texts which speak of Haxañ, that is, of Chinese Buddhists. Why do they speak of Chinese Buddhism? To negate it, to attack it, to debate it. But they never stop to explain clearly what is the principle of this Chinese Buddhist teaching that they are attacking. But in this book, the *Sàmdan Migdrŏn*, these concepts and principles are explained very clearly, since this teacher really had a knowledge of that Chinese teaching. He had, in fact, done a great deal of study and was a scholar of the development of the Chinese school, which can be considered as antagonistic to the school of gradual realization. Tibetan historians always speak of the council of Lhasa, and they always say that the great Indian master Kamalaśīla had been invited to come there and debate with Haxañ Mahāyāna, the Chinese representative, who was defeated and left in disgrace.[13] Many people give a great deal of importance to the texts of Kamalaśīla surrounding this controversy,[14] and it is true that they are very important from the point of view of the gradualist school. But it is not really the truth that is said in all those Tibetan polemical texts, because the major emphasis there is negating and debating with the Chinese proponent of the non-gradual approach. In fact, there is no real attempt to explain the position of Haxañ.

In general, we have this way of seeing according to the two truths, and when we speak of a school like that of Kamalaśīla, it is considered that through study, through preparation, through *xinas (zhi gnas, śamatha)* that, for example, in order to overcome wrath, one concentrates on compassion. Gradually through such effort one arrives at the condition of *midogba (mi rtog pa, nirvikalpa)*, that is, not being disturbed by thought. Thus, it is implied that one works to the maximum on the relative condition; then gradually through that, one arrives at the absolute truth. The system of the Chinese Buddhists, on the other hand, was not invented or created by them, but they had followed and taken their inspiration, above all, from certain sutras like the *Laṅkāvatāra*.[15] There exists a saying in that particular sutra about a person who from the beginning makes

24

efforts to reach the absolute truth; this principle, that a person should from the beginning aim at the absolute truth, is the same principle that was explained and expounded by the Chinese representative in Tibet, Haxañ Mahāyāna. He had represented the eleventh person in the lineal descent from the person who had introduced that particular knowledge and outlook known as Ch'an into China. In the text that I referred to, the *Sàmdan Migdrŏn*, these ten prior masters who had introduced and expounded the notion of aiming at the absolute condition from the beginning, are each presented, explained, and quoted in the fifth chapter.

Their principle is something very simple. If one does not have thoughts, for example, then the object of thought does not exist. If there is no object, then there is also no thought. That is to say, both are relative. But when both are relative you find yourself in the absolute condition. This is not a way of proceeding through a method of reasoning which seeks to define or carry one to nothingness, *śūnyatā*. But in the non-gradual approach one attempts to find oneself through practice, experientially, in the non-dual, and this is what they meant by finding oneself in a state undisturbed by thought, which is the genuinely absolute truth or condition. In fact, the system of Haxañ insisted a great deal on this concept; he explained that if one finds oneself in such a condition, then one has no need of a teaching, of a method, or a rule at all. Note: *if* one finds oneself in that condition. Then, he continues, if one finds oneself in that condition and a thought arises, good and evil are the same thing. He gives the example of a white cloud and a black cloud being the same thing in regard to covering the sun. But this kind of outlook never pleased all those schools who followed the example of Kamalaśīla, because all of the teachings of Kamalaśīla insisted that by working through the relative, developing oneself in the relative, one eventually arrives at the absolute condition.

On this point the Zógqen teaching is very similar to that of the Chinese Ch'an Buddhists. In the Zógqen teachings, too, there exists this same explanation of the relativity of good and bad. But this does not mean in Zógqen that one renounces or neglects the relative condition. As I said, *if* you find yourself in this absolute condition; but if you do not find yourself in this condition, you obviously do not just neglect relative matters. Thus, one can understand that the principle method of Zen is a way to find yourself in the absolute condition. This principle is a common element between Chinese Buddhism and Zógqen. But you must not therefore think they are one and the same thing. You must never forget that the two methods are different. We have already spoken of one as the way of self-liberation and the other as the path of renunciation. From the beginning, in principle, these two methods are very different.

When we speak of a teaching, a teaching always has a basis, then its path, and then its realization or outcome. The Zógqen teaching has also been called the teaching of self-perfectedness. This refers to the individual himself as self-perfected. The goal of the Zógqen teaching is not to arrive at the point of *śūnyatā* or void. In sutric Buddhism, in general the aim is *śūnyatā* or void, which means to aim oneself at what we call the absolute truth. In this text, the *Sàmdan Migdrön*, there is a very clear example given, as follows: when seeds have fallen on the ground and you are busy collecting the seeds, you are not looking at the earth. When you are looking for them, you are aiming, you are focused on the seeds, not the earth. Another example that is given is when you are trying to put a thread through a needle and you do not see the hole well. So you put it up to the sky against the light, in order to put the thread through. While your face and your eyes may be directed toward the sky, you are not seeing the sky, but are looking at the hole in the needle.[16] These are very clear examples. These are examples that make you understand clearly what is meant when we say that one is pointed towards the two truths or pointed towards *śūnyatā*.

This is also a very good way of understanding that method of transformation which we spoke of as Tantrism.[17] Tantrism in general is the path of transformation. It is not a path of renunciation. When there is a method for transforming things, it also means there is a method for integrating them. To go back to our example of seeds on the ground, in this case one is not staring, looking for the seeds, one is looking at the earth. The earth here is symbolic of our primordial condition, also known as *tantra*. But you also have to remember that the method of transformation takes place through, and depends upon, concentration. In order to accomplish this it may involve creation of many, many different means. If one wants to transform a dimension like this location, this building, and transform it into something else, one must first of all concentrate. In transformation practice this concentration has to become real for that person. When this transformation has become real, then *śūnyatā*, the void, has automatically been realized. It is not that *śūnyatā*, void, is a target at which one must aim, toward which one must direct oneself. It is rather that there is more to *śūnyatā* than the emptiness of the sutras; there is already a living manifestation. Then, through the capacity to have this manifestation present, that is, through the manifestation of the *maṇḍala*, the dimension of the peaceful and wrathful divinities, benefit is given to other beings. This is particular to the way of transformation, Tantrism.

From the point of view of Zógqen, however, this too is a form of gradual path, because in the teaching of Zógqen the principle is that of self-perfectedness. Self-perfectedness means that the so-called objective is nothing else than the manifestation of the energy of the primordial state of the individual himself. An individual who practices Zógqen must possess clear knowledge of the principle of energy and what it means. The principle of the Zógqen teaching is the self-perfectedness, the already-being-perfect of every individual. Another way of saying this is that the primordial state of the individual, one's actual condition, is explained as having an essence, nature, and energy.[18] Through these three, the essence, nature and energy, it is also explained how the three bodies, *trikāya*, ultimately manifest themselves. This manifestation is explained through what we speak of as energy. The way of manifesting energy can be either as subject or as object. In this regard we speak of *zal (rtsal)* and *rolba (rol pa)*, two ways in which energy can manifest.[19] Just having an intellectual concept of energy is not enough, but

27

one actually applies this knowledge of energy in practice. Through making use of one's own energy, one arrives at what we call "total realization." Thus, when one speaks of Zen and Zógqen, it is obvious that these two methods are very different and not to be confused with one another.

To better understand this explanation of energy and how it works, let us talk more about that energy which we call *zal*. *Zal* refers to the way in which energy manifests as an object. To use the example of a crystal, we put a crystal where a ray of sunlight falls and see everywhere in the room a series of manifestations of light in all the colors of the rainbow. In this case one should think that the crystal represents the state of the individual, that state which is already perfected from the very beginning. Now, if from that crystal arise all of these different colored lights, this is a way of understanding how our way of seeing things manifests itself, whether it be pure or impure vision. When we speak of pure vision, an individual knows or has the capacity to see, or perceive directly, the essence of the five elements, presenting themselves in the form of colors. When we speak of impure vision, an individual gives consideration to materiality rather than to the essence of the elements, which is light. Both of these, the pure and impure vision, are always the energy of the individual himself at work. The light that springs from the crystal presenting itself perhaps in different colors is still always light coming out of that crystal. This discussion has been given in order to understand at least one way in which energy manifests.

Another way in which energy manifests itself is called *rolba*. Here things manifest as if they were in the subject, subjectively. It is as if one were looking into a mirror. Here we should think that our primordial state is like a mirror. Anything which may find itself before the mirror can be reflected there. At this level of looking at the mirror from elsewhere, what might be reflected could be beautiful or ugly. But beautiful and ugly reflections make no difference to the mirror itself, and what is in the mirror cannot manifest outside of the mirror and its capacity to reflect. This we speak of as *rolba*, which is another way in which energy manifests itself. When we practice the way of transformation, for example, we concentrate on many, many things outside of our real, present condition. Whatever we are concentrating on using tantric methods, no matter how grandiose and splendid it may be, is still a manifestation of our energy which is *rolba*. Many people think that, when they are doing certain types of visualization, it is a kind of fantasy. It is true that it is a kind of fantasy, but it is a kind of fantasy which becomes real. Why can it become real? Because the level of energy as *rolba* belongs to the primordial state of the individual. Therefore it is very important for the Zógqen practitioner to know how to use this energy. When you know how to use your energy as it manifests, there is nothing to renounce. To have a clear or precise idea of the way of self-liberation, and to understand why it is different from the way of transformation, there is an example that is always used to exemplify or clarify this point. It is said that there is a way to make use of even the worst poison, so that it becomes medicine. This is an example given to illustrate the path of transformation. However, when we come to the Zógqen teaching, we see that the principle is based on how the energy of any object arises, whether it be material or immaterial. Energy is found at the level of *zal* or of *rolba*. When one has this knowledge and finds oneself in this state of experiencing everything as these energies, then there is nothing to transform.

It is obvious that if you do not find yourself at that level, I am not saying that at that point there is no use for transformation. Take the example of anger. In the Buddhist sutras it says that when one wants to overcome anger one must counter it by compassion. Maybe one does not succeed in being compassionate in that moment of anger. It might be that to reach a level of compassion, one needs to think and reason about it — one might have to think about the consequences of anger by thinking about the meaning and conditions of karma. It is said, for example, that all beings are our parents or have been our parents. The implication is that any given being may have been at times our father or our son, that there is no limitation to the infinity of transmigrations we have all been through. So, one might use all these different kinds of reasoning to cause the arising of a degree of compassion, and through this one drives away the anger that one had been experiencing. On the other hand, in Tantrism, there exists something quite different — for example, visualization of oneself as a wrathful deity. Instead of going into angry conflict with someone, one takes that energy to transform it and arrive at another dimension where that energy functions differently. For example, if I am arguing with somebody, that somebody is not going to be big enough to confront a manifestation of some kind of wrathful deity. It is better in this case to manifest myself as a wrathful being that can shake the entire universe rather that to just concentrate on threatening some individual. This is an example of the way in which we could use transformation.

When we speak of the path of self-liberation, there is neither a concept of renunciation, because if it is always my energy manifesting, then it can manifest in many different ways; nor is there a concept of transformation, because the principle here is that I find myself in a state of pure presence, of contemplation. If I find myself for an instant in a state of contemplation, then from that point of view, wrath and compassion are one and the same. Good and evil are one and the same. In that condition there is nothing to do; one liberates oneself, because one finds oneself in one's own dimension of energy without escaping and without renouncing anything. This is the principle of what is called the way of self-liberation. It does not mean that we must do something and thus create its consequences. Nor does it mean to not do and block our thoughts. To do something or not do something are the same — they are on the same level of action. This does not mean that one loses oneself distractedly in self-abandonment, without a state of presence.

We have a very important example of a great master, Yúñdon Dórje Bal (gYung ston rdo rje dpal), who was a great Zógqen master.[20] One day a visitor came to him, and said, "You Zógqen practitioners, you're always doing meditation, right?" And the master replied to him, "What am I supposed to be meditating on?," because meditating already implies that you are doing something, that there is some kind of concept involved. "Ah," said the visitor, "then you practitioners of Zógqen do not meditate?" And this time the master replied, "When am I ever distracted?" In these two answers you can also find the conclusion of Zógqen. If someone has a knowledge of what the teaching is about and applies it minimally, and takes it to this level, that can be called Zógqen, the self-perfected state of the individual.

The world where we find ourselves, the human dimension, is one's own energy. One has to know how to use that energy, know how to find it in the same dimension as one's own primordial state. It is clear that you have to do a little work to arrive at that point; otherwise you cannot quite live it. So if you have done a little work, a minimum of work on this, and begun to experience what is as your own energy, then you can understand. In that case you could begin to understand what is meant here by neither doing something, that is, creating an action with all its consequences, nor being distracted. Thus you develop what is called contemplation.

Footnotes

1. On these issues see Namkhai Norbu, *The Necklace of Zi, A Cultural History of Tibet* (Dharamsala: Information Office of His Holiness the Dalai Lama, 1981).

2. On the early Tibetan Kings, see Stein, R.A., *Tibetan Civilization* (Stanford: Stanford University Press, 1972), Ch. II.

3. See for example, Namkhai Norbu, *Zhang Bod Lo Rgyus: La Storia Antica dello Zhang Zhung e del Tibet* (Napoli: Comunità Dzogchen, 1981), pp. 225-33.

4. See N. Norbu, *Bod kyi lo rgyus las 'phros pa'i gtam nor bu'i do shal* (Dharamsala: Library of Tibetan Works and Archives, 1981), p. 27 ff; Per Kvaerne, " 'The Great Perfection' in the tradition of the Bonpos", in *Early Ch'an in China and Tibet*, Lancaster, L. & Lai, W., Eds. (Berkeley: Berkeley Buddhist Studies Series 5, 1983), pp. 368-69.

5. Dunhuang was an important center of Buddhism in the Tang period, being located on the silk route. At the end of the last century, European scholars discovered there a valuable cache of texts in Chinese, Tibetan, and other Central Asian languages.

6. It is commonly held in Tibet that only a few *Kriyā Tantras* were transmitted by Śākyamuni as *Nirmāṇakāya*, the rest being transmissions of the *Sambhoga-kāya*, that is, manifestations through transformation into a *maṇḍala*.

7. On *Sem sde* and *Klong sde* see N. Norbu & K. Lipman, *Primordial Experience: Mañjuśrīmitra's Treatise on the Meaning of Bodhicitta in rDzogs chen* (Delhi: Motilal Banarsidass, forthcoming), Introduction. Briefly, the *Sems sde* works primarily according to the presentation of what is common to Buddhism. That is to say, it presents itself in a way more easily understood by those who are steeped in Buddhism and Buddhist philosophy. It could also be said that the *Sems sde* uses the methods which, above all, take you to a knowledge of contemplation through intellectual steps. Compared to the *Klong sde*, the *Sems sde* seems more like a gradual method. The *Klong sde* teaching proceeds more directly into practice. You can also think about these two in terms of the three final sayings of dGa' rab rdo rje, the *Tshig gsum gnad brdegs*. The concern of the *Sems sde* is more that of the first saying, "direct introduction" to one's primordial state, for one who has not had such an introduction, while the *Klong sde* works more on the second saying, "not remaining in doubt." This means to experience thoroughly and unquestionably for oneself what one has been introduced to.

8. Nowadays, rDzogs chen is usually taught according to *gter ma* such as the *Klong chen snying thig* of 'Jigs med gling pa.

9. See E. Dargyay, *The Rise of Esoteric Buddhism in Tibet* (Delhi: Motilal Banarsidass, 1977), p. 57-58.

10. The Ch'an school traces itself back from the master who was said to have introduced it into China, Bodhidharma, to Kāśyapa. See *Early Ch'an in China and*

Tibet for many discussions of the Ch'an lineage.

11. *Bsam gtam mig sgron* (Leh, Ladakh: S.W. Tashigangpa, 1974), p. 23-24: Kamalaśīla taught according to sutras which were provisional in their meaning *(drang don)* and "incomplete" *(yongs su ma rdzogs)*, while Ha shang taught according to sutras which were "complete" *(yongs su rdzogs)*. See H.V. Guenther, " 'Meditation' Trends in Early Tibet," in *Early Ch'an in China and Tibet*, p. 352. There is a parallel passage in the *bKa' thang sde lnga*, edited and translated by G. Tucci in his *Minor Buddhist Texts* (Rome: Is. M.E.O., 1958), p. 68 f. He mistranslates, "The Indian acārya Kamalaśīla did not fully realize (the meaning) of the sutras, the sense of which is to be determined (i.e., relative, *drang don, neyārtha)* . . ." (p. 82, the passage in Tibetan is to be found on p. 69). The text has the same meaning as that of the *Bsam gtan mig sgron*.

12. See note above. With this authentic text of the early period we can resolve many of the confusions created by trying to piece together an understanding of the controversies surrounding Ha shang Mahāyāna from later sources, as was done by Tucci. We agree with Per Kvaerne: "Tucci, in spite of his repeated assertions that Ch'an elements are to be found in Rdzogs-chen, nowhere demonstrates that these elements must necessarily, or even preferably, be interpreted as emanating from Ch'an. Nevertheless, subsequent writers, when dealing with the question, speak of Ch'an elements in Rdzogs-chen as if this were an established fact, and refer to Tucci. . . . The question of the continued presence of Ch'an in Tibet after the eighth to ninth centuries, would therefore seem to be more appropriately dealt with independently of Rdzogs-chen. Discussing this question, S.G. Karmay concludes (Karmay, "A General Introduction to the History and Doctrines of Bon," *Memoirs of the Research Department of the Toyo Bunko*, No. 33, Tokyo, 1975, p. 215) that 'even though in rDzogs-chen there may be parallel ideas and practices to those of Ch'an, rDzogs-chen must be considered as of Indo-Tibetan origin whilst the tradition of Ch'an in Tibet may be studied as an independent movement' " *(Early Ch'an in China and Tibet*, pp. 384-85).

13. For a critical assessment of the "debate" see Yoshiro Imaeda, "Documents Tibetains de Touen-houang Concernant Le Council du Tibet," *Journal Asiatique*, Fasc. 1 and 2, 1975, pp. 125-46. Uncritical acceptance of the later Tibetan sources still continues among western scholars; see, for example, G. Houston, "The Bsam Yas Debate: According to the Rgyal Rabs Gsal Ba'i Me Long," *Central Asiatic Journal*, vol. xviii, no. 4, 1974, pp. 209-16.

14. These are the three *Bhāvanākrama*. See Tucci, *Minor Buddhist Texts*, Part II, and Part III (Rome: Is. M.E.O., 1971).

15. See D.T. Suzuki, *Laṅkāvatāra Sūtra* (London: Routledge & Kegan Paul, 1968) and *Studies in the Laṅkāvatāra Sūtra* (London: Routledge & Kegan Paul, 1968).

16. *Bsam gtan mig sgron*, p. 62.

17. On the way of transformation *(sgyur lam)*, see *Primordial Experience*, Preface and Introduction.

18. On essence *(ngo bo)*, nature *(rang bzhin)* and energy *(thugs rje)*, see H.V.

Guenther, *Kindly Bent to Ease Us, Part One: Mind* (Emeryville, CA: Dharma Press, 1975), Introduction; *Tibetan Buddhism in Western Perspective* (Emeryville, CA: Dharma Press, 1977), pp. 119, 124-25, 156, 176, 212. Guenther uses the terms "facticity," "actuality," and "responsiveness." One may explain these three in terms of one's thought process and its observation. Thoughts in their "essence," when examined as to their origin, presence, and cessation, cannot be located and affirmed, and are thus "void" *(stong pa)*. Yet they continue, and this is their "nature," which is a kind of "radiance" or "clarity" *(gsal ba)*. In this continuing radiance, thoughts also have their characteristic "energy," which is their incessant *(ma 'gags pa)* power to lead us into either judgment and karmic action, or to maintaining a state of pure presence *(rig pa)* without judgment, no matter how this "energy" manifests itself.

Sutric teachings, by aiming at an experience of *śūnyatā*, primarily cultivate the first facet, "essence." Tantric teachings work primarily with the second facet, "nature" as radiant presence; or, more precisely stated, the unity of the first two facets *(stong gsal)*. Zógqen explains that its basis *(gzhi)*, the primordial state of the individual, *is* all three together; through this understanding it has special methods, such as the practice of *thod rgal*, for working with the third facet, "energy."

19. On *rtsal* and *rol pa*, see Norbu & Lipman, *Primordial Experience*, op. cit., Introduction. A third form of "energy" is usually also mentioned in the texts of rDzogs chen, either *gdangs* or *rgyan*. *gDangs* indicates a manifestation which is neither subjective nor objective; *rgyan* means that the energy is experienced as an "ornament" to one's primordial state.

20. G.yung ston rdo rje dpal (1284-1365) was a contemporary of Klong chen rab 'byams pa and the third Karma pa, Rang byung rdo rje.

Biographical Sketch of the Author

The author of this text on rDzogs chen practice, Nam mkha'i Norbu Rinpoche, was born in the village of dGe'ug, in the lCong ra district of sDe dge in East Tibet, on the eighth day of the tenth month of the Earth-Tiger year (1938). His father was sGrol ma Tshe ring, member of a noble family and sometime official with the government of sDe dge, and his mother was Ye shes Chos sgron.

When he was two years old, dPal yul Karma Yang srid Rinpoche[1] and Zhe chen Rab byams Rinpoche,[2] both recognized him as the reincarnation of A'dzom 'Brug pa.[3] A 'dzom 'Brug pa was one of the great rDzogs chen Masters of the early part of this century. He was the disciple of the first mKhyen brtse Rinpoche, 'Jam dbyangs mKhyen brtse dBang po (1829-1892), and also the disciple of dPal sprul Rinpoche.[4] Both of these illustrious teachers were leaders of the *Ris med* or non-sectarian movement in nineteenth-century eastern Tibet. On some thirty-seven occasions, A'dzom 'Brug pa received transmissions from his principal master, 'Jam dbyangs mKhyen brtse, and from dPal sprul Rinpoche he received the complete transmissions of the *kLong chen snying thig* and the *rTsa rlung* precepts. In turn, A'dzom 'Brug pa became a *gter ston*, or discoverer of hidden treasure texts, having received visions directly from the incomparable 'Jigs med gLing pa (1730-1798) when the former was thirty. Teaching at A 'dzom sgar in eastern Tibet during summer and winter retreats,[5] A'dzom 'Brug pa became the master of many contemporary teachers of rDzogs chen. Among them was Norbu Rinpoche's paternal uncle, rTogs ldan O rgyan bsTan 'dzin,[6] who was his first rDzogs chen teacher.

When he was eight years old, the sixteenth Karmapa,[7] and dPal spung Situ Rinpoche[8] both recognized Norbu Rinpoche to be the mind-incarnation[9] of Lho 'Brug Zhabs drung Rinpoche.[10] This latter master, the reincarnation of the illustrious 'Brug pa bKa' brgyud master, Padma dKar po (1527-1592), was the actual historical founder of the state of Bhutan. Until the early twentieth century, the Zhabs drung Rinpoches were the Dharmarajas or temporal and spiritual rulers of Bhutan.

While yet a child, from rDzogs chen mKhan Rinpoche,[11] from his maternal uncle mKhyen brtse Yang srid Rinpoche,[12] and from his paternal uncle rTogs ldan O rgyan bsTan 'dzin, Norbu Rinpoche received instruction in the *rDzogs chen gsang ba snying thig* and the *sNying thig Yab bzhi*. Meanwhile, from gNas rgyab mChog sprul Rinpoche,[13] he received the transmissions of the *rNying ma bka' ma*, the *kLong gsal rdo rje snying po*, and the *gNam chos* of Mi 'gyur rDo rje. From mKhan Rinpoche dPal ldan Tshul khrims (1906-) he received the transmissions from the *rGyud sde kun btus*, the famous Sa skya pa collection of tantric practices. And in addition, he received many initiations and listened to many oral explanations[14] from famous Ris med pa or nonsectarian masters of eastern Tibet.

From the time he was eight years old until he was twelve, he attended the college of sDe dge dbon stod slob grwa at sDe dge dgon chen Monastery, where, with mKhen Rinpoche mKhyen rab Chos kyi 'od zer (1901-), he studied the thirteen basic texts[15] used in the standard academic curriculum designed by mKhan po gZhan dga'.[16] Norbu Rinpoche became especially expert in the *Abhisamayālaṅkāra*. In addition, with this same master he studied the great commentary to the *Kālacakra Tantra*,[17] the *Guhyagarbha Tantra*, the *Zab mo nang don* of Karmapa Rang byung rDo rje, the Medical Tantras,[18] Indian and Chinese astrology,[19] as well as receiving from him the initiations and transmissions of the *Sa skya'i sgrub thabs kun btus.*

From the age of eight until he was fourteen, at the college of sDe dge Ku se gSer ljongs bshad grwa, from mKhan Rinpoche Brag gyab Blos gros (1913-), he received instructions in the *Prajñāpāramitā sutras*, the *Abhisamayā-laṅkāra*, and three tantric texts: the *rDorje Gur*, the *Hevajra Tantra* and the *Samputa Tantra*.[20] By his tutor mChog sprul Rinpoche[21] he was instructed in the secular sciences.[22]

Also, from the age of eight until he was fourteen, having gone to rDzong gsar Monastery in eastern Tibet, he received teachings from the illustrious rDzong gsar mKhyen brtse Rinpoche[23] on the *Sa skya'i zab chos lam 'bras*, the quintessential doctrine of the Sa skya pa school and, in addition, on the three texts: *rGyud kyi spyi don rnam bzhag*, *lJon shing chen mo*, and the *Hevajra Tantra*. [24] Then at the college of Khams bre bshad grwa, with mKhan Rinpoche Mi nyag Dam chos (1920-) he studied a basic text on logic, the *Tshad ma rig gter* of Sa skya Paṇḍita.

Then, in the meditation cave at Seng-chen gNam brag, he made a retreat with his uncle the rTogs ldan O rgyan bsTan 'dzin for the practices of Vajrapāṇi, Siṃhamukha, and White Tārā. At that time, the son of A'dzom 'Brug pa, 'Gyur med rDo rje (1895-), returned from Central Tibet, and staying with them, the latter bestowed the cycle of *rDo rje gro lod*, the *Klong chen snying thig*, and the cycle of the *dGongs pa zang thal* of Rig 'dzin rGod ldem 'Phru can.

When he was fourteen years old in 1951, he received the initiations for Vajrayogini according to the Ngor pa and Tshar pa traditions of the Sa skya. Then his tutor advised him to seek out a woman living in the Kadari region who was the living embodiment of Vajrayogini herself and take initiation from her. This woman master, A yo mKha' 'gro rDo rje dPal sgron (1838-1953), was a direct disciple of the great 'Jam dbyangs mKhyen brtse dBang po and of Nyag bla Padma bDud 'dul, as well as being an elder contemporary of A 'dzom 'Brug pa. At this time she was one hundred and thirteen years old and had been in a dark retreat[25] for some fifty-six years. Norbu Rinpoche received from her transmissions for the *mKha' 'gro gsang 'dus*, the mind-treasure[26] of 'Jam dbyangs mKhyen brtse dBang po, and the *mKha' 'gro yang thig*, in which the principal practice is the dark retreat, as well as the *Klong chen snying thig*. She also bestowed upon him her own mind-treasures, including that for the Ḍākinī Siṃhamukha, the *mKha' 'gro dbang mo'i seng ge gdong ma'i zab thig*.

Then in 1954, he was invited to visit the People's Republic of China as a representative of Tibetan youth. From 1954 he was an instructor in Tibetan language at the Southwestern University of Minor Nationalities at Chengdu, Sichuan, China. While living in China, he met the famous Gangs dkar Rinpoche.[27] From the master he heard many explanations of the Six Doctrines of Nāropa,[28] Mahāmudrā, the *dKon mchog spyi 'dus*, as well as Tibetan medicine. During this time, Norbu Rinpoche also acquired proficiency in the Chinese and Mongolian languages.

When he was seventeen years old, returning to his home country of sDe dge following a vision received in dream, he came to meet his Root Master,[29] Nyag bla Rinpoche Rig 'dzin Byang chub rDo rje (1826-1978), who lived in a remote valley to the east of sDe gde. Byang chub rDo rje Rinpoche hailed originally from the Nyag rong region on the borders of China. He was a disciple of A 'dzom 'Brug pa, of Nyag bla Padma bDud 'dul, and of Shar rdza Rinpoche,[30] the famous Bonpo teacher of rDzogs chen who attained the Rainbow Body of Light.[31] A practicing physician, Byang chub rDo rje Rinpoche headed a commune called Nyag bla sGar in this remote valley; it was a totally self-supporting community consisting entirely of lay practitioners, yogins and yoginis. From this master, Norbu Rinpoche received initiation into, and transmission of, the essential teachings of rDzogs chen *Sems sde, Klong sde*, and *Man ngag gi sde*. More importantly, this master introduced him directly to the experience of rDzogs chen. He remained here for almost a year, often assisting Byang chub rDo rje Rinpoche in his medical practice and serving as his scribe and secretary. He also received transmissions from the master's son, Nyag sras 'Gyur med rDo rje.

After this, Norbu Rinpoche set out on a prolonged pilgrimage to Central Tibet, Nepal, India, and Bhutan. Returning to sDe dge, the land of his birth, he found that deteriorating political conditions had led to the eruption of violence. Fleeing first toward Central Tibet, he finally emerged safely in Sikkim as a refugee. From 1958 to 1960 he lived in Gangtok, Sikkim, employed as an author and editor of Tibetan text books for the Development Office, the Government of Sikkim. In 1960 when he was twenty-two years old, at the invitation of Professor Giuseppe Tucci, he went to Italy and resided for several years in Rome. During this time, from 1960 to 1964, he was a research associate at the Istituto Italiano per il Medio ed Estremo Oriente. Receiving a grant from the Rockefeller Foundation, he worked in close collaboration with

Professor Tucci, and wrote two appendices to Professor Tucci's *Tibetan Folk Songs of Gyantse and Western Tibet* (Rome, 1966), as well as giving seminars at IsMEO on yoga, medicine, and astrology.

From 1964 to the present, Norbu Rinpoche has been a professor at the Istituto Orientale, University of Naples, where he teaches Tibetan language, Mongolian language, and Tibetan cultural history. Since then he has done extensive research into the historical origins of Tibetan culture, investigating little-known literary sources from the Bonpo tradition. In 1983, Norbu Rinpoche hosted the first International Convention on Tibetan Medicine held at Venice, Italy. Although still actively teaching at the university, for the past ten years Norbu Rinpoche has informally conducted teaching retreats in various countries, including Italy, France, England, Austria, Denmark, Norway, Finland, and since 1979, the United States. During these retreats, he gives practical instruction in rDzogs chen practices in a non-sectarian format, as well as teaching aspects of Tibetan culture, especially Yantra Yoga, Tibetan medicine and astrology. Moreover, under his guidance there has grown up, at first in Italy and now in several other countries, including the United States, what has come to be known as the Dzogchen Community.[32] This is an informal association of individuals who, while continuing to work at their usual occupations in society, share a common interest in pursuing and practicing the teachings which Norbu Rinpoche continues to transmit.

The above information was largely extracted by John Reynolds from a biography in Tibetan appended to Professor Norbu's *gZi yi Phreng ba* (Dharamsala: Library of Tibetan Works and Archives, 1982).

Notes to the Biography

1. Kun-bzang 'gro 'dul 'od gsal klong yangs rdo rje, 1898- .

2. sNang mdzod grub pa'i rdo rje, 1900- .

3. 'Gro 'dul dpa' bo rdo rje, 1842-1924.

4. rDza dPal sprul Rin po che, O rgyan 'jigs med chos kyi dbang po, 1808-87.

5. During summer retreats he taught rDzogs chen and during winter retreats he taught *rtsa rlung*, the yoga of the channels and energies.

6. The term *rtogs ldan* means "one who has attained understanding," and is more or less synonymous with *rnal 'byor pa*, "a yogin."

7. rGyal ba Karmapa, Rang 'byung rig pa'i rdo rje, 1924-81.

8. Padma dbang mchog rgyal po, 1886-1952.

9. thugs kyi sprul sku.

10. Ngag dbang rnam rgyal, 1594-1651.

11. Kun dga' dpal ldan, 1878-1950.

12. 'Jam dbyangs chos kyi dbang phyug, 1910-73.
13. 'Jam dbyangs blo gros rgya mtsho, 1902-52.
14. dbang dang khrid.
15. *gzhung chen bcu gsum.* These texts are:
    1. *Prātimokṣa sūtra*
    2. *Vinaya sūtra* by Gunaprabha
    3. *Abhidharmasamuccaya* by Asaṅga
    4. *Abhidharmakoṣa* by Vasubandhu
    5. *Mūlamadhyamakakārikā* by Nāgārjuna
    6. *Madhyamakāvatāra* by Candrakīrti
    7. *Catuḥśataka* by Āryadeva
    8. *Bodhicaryāvatāra* by Śāntideva
    9. *Abhisamayālaṅkāra* by Maitreya/Asanga
    10. *Mahāyānasūtrālaṅkāra* by Maitreya/Asanga
    11. *Madhyāntavibhaṅga* by Maitreya/Asanga
    12. *Dharmadharmatāvibhaṅga* by Maitreya/Asanga
    13. *Uttaratantra* by Maitreya/Asanga
16. gZhan phan chos kyi snang ba.
17. Dus 'khor 'grel chen.
18. *rGyud bzhi.*
19. *rtsis dkar nag.*
20. *gur brtag sam gsum.*
21. Yongs 'dzin mchog sprul, Kun dga' grags pa, 1922- .
22. *rig gnas kyi skor.*
23. rDzong gsar mkhyen brtse Rin po che, Jam mgon mkhyen sprul Chos kyi blo gros, 1896-1959.
24. *spyi ljon brtag gsum.* The *Hevajra Tantra* is also known as the *brtag gnyis* because it is divided into two parts.
25. *mun mtshams.*
26. *dgongs gter.*
27. Gangs dkar Rin po che, Karma bshad sprul Chos kyi seng ge, 1903-56.
28. Na ro chos drug.
29. rtsa ba'i bla ma.
30. Shar rdza bKra shis rgyal mtshan, 1859-1935.
31. *'ja' lus pa.*
32. *rdzogs chen 'dus sde.*

Books by Namkhai Norbu

1. *Manuale di lingua tibetana* (Naples: Comunità Dzogchen, 1977): an introductory grammar and reader of Tibetan language (in Italian).

2. *Zhang Bod Lo rgyrus* (Naples: Comunità Dzogchen, 1981): a collection of texts dealing with the ancient history of Zhang zhung and Tibet (in Tibetan and Italian).

3. *Bod kyi lo rgyrus las'phros pa'i gtam nor bu'i do shal* (Dharamsala: Library of Tibetan Works and Archives, 1981): a new interpretation of ancient Tibetan history and culture (in Tibetan).

4. *The Necklace of gZi: A Cultural History of Tibet* (Dharamsala: Library of Tibetan Works and Archives, 1981): an investigation of the origins of Tibetan culture in the ancient civilization of Zhang Zhung.

5. *gZi yi phren ba* (Dharamsala: Library of Tibetan Works and Archives, 1982): Tibetan text of the above.

6. *Yantra Yoga* (Naples: Comunità Dzogchen 1982): a treatise on the classical system of Yantra Yoga of Vairocana (in Tibetan).

7. *Byang 'brog lam yig* (Arcidosso: Shang Shung Edizioni, 1983): an account of the culture of the nomadic tribes of North Tibet (in Tibetan).

8. *On Birth and Life: A Treatise on Tibetan Medicine* (Venice: Shang Shung Edizioni, 1983): a summary of Tibetan medicine.

9. *The Mirror: Advice on Presence and Awareness* (Arcidosso: Shang Shung Edizioni, 1983): an introduction to Dzogchen practice.

10. *Primordial Experience: Mañjuśrīmitra's Treatise on the Meaning of Bodhicitta in rDzogs chen*, with K. Lipman, in collaboration with B. Simmons (Boston: Shambhala Publications, 1986).

OTHER TITLES
FROM BLUE DOLPHIN PUBLISHING

The Inner Palace
Mirrors of Psychospirituality in
Divine and Sacred Wisdom-Traditions
Mitchell D. Ginsberg, Ph.D.
2 Vol. set: paperback, $59.95, ISBN: 1-57733-136-2, hardcover, $99.95,
ISBN: 1-57733-137-0; Vol. 1, 404 pp., Vol. 2, 474 pp.

Turning to the Source
An Eastern View of Western Mind: Using Insight Meditation and
Psychotherapy for Personal Growth, Health and Wholeness
Dhiravamsa
ISBN: 0-931892-20-1, 256 pp., 6.25 x 9.25, hardcover, $19.95

The Middle Path of Life
Talks on the Practice of Insight Meditation
Dhiravamsa
ISBN: 0-931892-22-8, 96 pp., 5.5 x 8.5, paper, $9.95

Cities of Lightning
The Iconography of Thunder-Beings in the Oriental Traditions
Samudranath
ISBN: 0-9660203-0-8, 216 pp., 8.5 x 11, paper, $24.95

The Science of the Soul
On Consciousness and the Structure of Reality
Geoffrey D. Falk
ISBN: 1-57733-131-1, 340 pp., 6 x 9, paper, $19.95

OTHER TITLES
FROM BLUE DOLPHIN PUBLISHING

Jellyfish Bones
The Humor of Zen

Zen Master Donald Gilbert

ISBN: 0-931892-21-X, 168 pages, 5.5 x 8.5, paper, $14.95

"Master Gilbert's book is a fresh approach to Zen. He does not adhere to tradition nor does he deny it. The work seems light and humorous, but his pen is a Zen sword and it is very sharp indeed.

"Humor is an integral part of Zen and here it is employed with consummate skill. Those who have studied under Master Gilbert know him for his gentle humanism. They know too that he can, in one flash of incisive wit, burst conceptual bubbles in a cascade of laughter.

"In the book be aware of the little dog with his bone. He is often depicted as saying, 'This bone is delicious.' This is a most important clue. This book, then, is a finger pointed at the moon. If the reader can stop staring at the finger and look at the moon, the moon will be revealed smiling back at the looker.

"When the little ego is recognized for what it is, then the Buddha will romp and play, filling the world with unimpeded laughter. Master Gilbert's book may just be the instrument that will help bring this about."

Ven. Dr. Seo Kyung Bo, Zen Master
of the Il Bung Son Won Sect in Korea,
Tripitaka (Scriptures) Master and
Master of Chan-pil Calligraphy

OTHER TITLES
FROM BLUE DOLPHIN PUBLISHING

The Planetary Mind
Becoming Fully Human in the 21st Century
Michael W. Simpson, Ph.D.
ISBN: 1-57733-130-3, 208 pp., 6 x 9, paper, $16.95

Entering the Diamond Way
Tibetan Buddhism Meets the West
Lama Ole Nydahl
ISBN: 0-931892-03-1, 240 pp., 5.5 x 8.5, paper, $14.95

Riding the Tiger
Twenty Years on the Road:
The Risks and Joys of Bringing Tibetan Buddhism to the West
Lama Ole Nydahl
ISBN: 0-931892-67-8, 512 pp., 5.5 x 8.5, paper, $17.95

The Way Things Are
A Living Approach to Buddhism for Today's World
Lama Ole Nydahl
ISBN: 0-931892-38-4, 96 pp., 5.5 x 8.5, paper, $10.00

Rogues in Robes
An Inside Chronicle of a Recent Chinese-Tibetan Intrigue
in the Karma Kagyu Lineage of Diamond Way Buddhism
Tomek Lehnert
ISBN: 1-57733-026-9, 336 pp., 5.5 x 8.5, paper, $16.95

Litigation as Spiritual Practice
George J. Felos
ISBN: 1-57733-104-4, 344 pp., 6 x 9, hardcover, $24.95

ORDERS: 1-800-643-0765 • WEB: www.bluedolphinpublishing.com

OTHER TITLES
FROM BLUE DOLPHIN PUBLISHING

Awakening Love
The Universal Mission: Spiritual Healing in Psychology and Medicine
Nicholas C. Demetry, M.D. & Edwin L. Clonts, M.D.
ISBN: 1-57733-075-7, 240 pp., 6 x 9, paper, $14.95

Edgework
Exploring the Psychology of Disease:
A Manual for Healing Beyond Diet & Fitness
Ronald L. Peters, M.D., M.P.H.
ISBN: 1-57733-116-8, 284 pp., 6 x 9, paper, $17.95

The Art of Letting Go
A Pathway to Inner Freedom
Vidya Frazier, L.C.S.W.
ISBN: 1-57733-112-5, 260 pp., 6 x 9, paper, $16.95

People of the Circle, People of the Four Directions
Scott McCarthy
ISBN: 1-57733-013-7, paper, 712 pp., 155 illus., 6 x 9, $34.95
ISBN: 1-57733-014-5, hardcover, $49.95

The Way It Is
One Water, One Air, One Mother Earth
Corbin Harney
ISBN: 0-931892-80-5, 268 pp., 101 photos, 6 x 9, paper, $16.00

Spirit Visions
The Old One Speak
Dennison & Teddi Tsosie
ISBN: 1-57733-002-1, 384 pp., 6 x 9, paper, $19.95

ORDERS: 1-800-643-0765 • WEB: www.bluedolphinpublishing.com